Saturn

coming out of its

Retrograde

Saturn

coming out of its

Retrograde

Briana Roldan

HEADMISTRESS PRESS

ISBN: 978-0-9995930-8-0

Cover art by Hilma af Klint, *The Dove, No. 12, Group IX/UW, No. 36*
(1915). Public Domain.
Cover & book design by Mary Meriam.

PUBLISHER
Headmistress Press
60 Shipview Lane
Sequim, WA 98382
Telephone: 917-428-8312
Email: headmistresspress@gmail.com
Website: headmistresspress.blogspot.com

Contents

Diversity in Normativity

I am from many places
So many that I can barely count.
From the pen and the paper
from oil paint to empty canvases
from Hispanic Islands to Bronx low-income housing
From a heritage I am almost ignorant of.
I am from mild agoraphobia, extreme anxiety and depression.
I am from days spent in my room because the outside presents too many things
That I cannot bare to face.
From Drug Addict Parents and from sisters who raised me.
I am from questions like "did you get outside today?"
"Do you feel like hurting yourself or others?"
"You're *really* a lesbian? Well, are you sure it's not a phase?"
"Non-binary? Preferred pronouns? You are clearly just a girl."
I am from hypersensitivity
that makes me cry at light
and absorb people's energies.
I am from places of uncertainty
places of misunderstanding
places of concrete.
Yet, from places of love.
From self-love
to friend love
to unexpected love
to a genderfluid love.
From a love made of beautiful scents, sweeter words, and poetry.

I am from a Maya Angelou and Octavio Paz love.

From sunsets

and moon phases

From soil

to grass

to flowers

to trees.

And of all the places that I find myself to be from

I am most importantly

from a place of universal love.

New Places

Here I am.
Here I am finding myself
Yet again
Erasing someone who I thought I knew.
Here I am
Falling like the leaves unintentionally again.
> Falling in new places
>> Places that are broken
>> Places that are healing
> Places that are
> Places that are screaming

Places that are dreaming of
>> You
>> Me
>> Them Too.

And Here I am
Disconnected from Reality
> Disconnected from You
Disconnected from this.
Here I am in new
> Highs
> and older Lows.
Here I am
> Here I am
Here I am
in this place yet again.

Shedding my leaves
in the hopes that you will water me
Breaking and bending
in the hopes that you will save me
Falling and crashing
in the hopes that you will catch me
Every night
living and dying
Waiting for you
Waiting for me
Waiting for them
Waiting for everything.
Here I am
Always Waiting.

To Fall and Love Falling

There we were in silence
             Resembling cutlery
As the leaves changed from
             Green to red
                 To yellow
       To orange
                 To brown.
And there we were
Driving through the state
Fall foliage 360 degrees.
It was beautiful
             Refreshing
          Breathtaking
Like the way the crescent moon illuminates
an empty yet, full room.
                    There we were
In the midst of live music
Surrounded by acres of pumpkin patches
          and wine
               and apple groves.
Surrounded by homemade pastries
and warm apple cider
                 and mums in a pot too small
               to contain their growth
             Like the way your eyes are too full of life
             to contain their love.

And there
there we were exchanging pleasantries
that no one else could ever understand.
And so, here we are
Falling into new places
places we love
places where we are endless.
And here we are growing like mums
in a pot too small for comfort
Yet, blooming like Sunflowers in the spring.
To fall and Love falling
Oh, what a beautiful thing.

Full Moon Eyes

When I met her
There were no fireworks when I walked in
No sparks when I took the seat next to her.
But she looked at me with these brown, full moon eyes.
Those full moon eyes
Those full moon eyes
That goddamn crescent moon smirk.
Her *I love you's* bounced off the walls of my chemically imbalanced brain
A dopamine rush.
We kissed
sharing the same breath
Within an empty, cold staircase.
And I
I was winding down
Spiraling
Drowning
Basking
Embracing
Falling
into those full moon eyes.
And when we found ourselves
walking back to where our feet had been so many times before
and when we smelled Autumn in the air
and when we laid in the grass once more
our souls spoke to each other in a sweet silence
louder than I could have ever imagined.

And All that remained was the way our heartbeats intertwined.

In comfortable silence

we went back

back to feeling limitless

back to feeling like there was no end

or beginning

and we would have rather exchanged emotions through

swollen lips and urgent hands.

Yet, we never had the intention of creating

such beauty

Such art

But those goddamn full moon eyes

Stripped me of all the poison the world ever fed my heart.

Those full moon eyes

Those brown, full moon eyes

mended each and every wound.

And those full moon eyes

Those full moon eyes taught me

How to love the universe within me

How to grow flowers through such thick concrete.

How to kiss every inch of myself softly.

Those full moon eyes taught me

how to paint masterpieces from all that we have

and that, that is each other.

Colliding Oceans

Poetry.
She whispers, she screams.
She creates waves within my ocean
And bursts endlessly through my every seam.
Flipping through her pages
Carefully re-reading every line
Drowning in all of her complexity
Flowing through mounds of Simplicity.
I feel her every breath against my skin
I feel her soft, silent kiss in the dead of night
And her small smile at sun rise.
I know her, I feel her
Flowing through me as I flow through her.
We create our own subtle language
Our own lines that pour into one another
Our own metaphors
Our own similes.
We create our whispering, screaming Poetry.

Lost My Brain in Flames

Please find my brain.

        With your blood soaked hands

            Oh, America help me

With your generous wave of funding into my very own mental illness.

With your dying need to address my mental health

        Could you, America, help me find my brain?

So selfish of me to ask

Oh, but where would I be if I were my brain?

        We don't talk about it anyhow.

But you say it's okay

            And then my brain went up in flames

10 PM cries

        2 AM smokes

            4 AM soliloquies

Where would you be if you were my brain?

        Could you please help me find my head again?

Injustice everywhere but

        Shootings here, shootings there

            Massacres of the Americas?

Oh, that can't be my brain!

        Where would I be if I were my brain?

        Help me, I've lost my head again.

When was the last time You've seen my brain?

        Out on the town?

            It seems that it's gone

        Help me, I've lost my head again, *America*.

Raised American

From the dining table, comfortable silence
        Middle class
        working class
poorer class.
What does it take to create?
The feeling of wealth burning at the back of your brain.
            But are you happy? Are you sane?
Does that burning sensation ever subside?
You were taught American Christianity
        Let us not forget Christopher Columbus
The man in search of spices
                An American Lie
        An American Lie
                An American Lie
                    With so much pride.
Is this all you have to offer?
You said that you were so much more than Green
But whispers are always flying around.
Feeding you the promise of life
the promise of happiness
        the promise of wealth
                through the power lines
                the power lines
                those goddamn power lines
For a small payment of your soul.
                Your soul

What does it take?

What does it take?

What will it take?

"There's a burning sensation at the back of my brain!"

you cry

you weep within all of your green.

Maniaque Euphorique

Shaking Hands
  Words racing down
      this
  trapdoor
How do I fathom colors that are brighter
  Ideas that are flying
      Where is the pin when you need it?
  The muzzle when you should use it?
      This is no LSD-induced trip
How do I describe this to a shrink
Go figure, maybe?
  Skipping pills
too small to miss
  Cry Baby holding the milk
Disorganized and probably a maniac
For sure a maniac
But really, I should accept myself
  With too many neurons in my synaptic cleft
  I am always changing
      Such simple fluctuations
Looking for inspiration
  in weird places
      in the depths of my brain
Through Euphoria
Through Shaking Hands
      Heavier Hearts

Who am I?
When colors are brighter
And
When I'm in front of a shrink
Not my usual self
  Just the simple fluctuations
    The simple repercussions
of a Chemical Imbalance
  A euphoric high
    A set of Shaking Hands
And a Beating Heart
  A mind that just can't stop.

Five AM Tribute

It is always difficult to write.
> The insides are always jumbled up
>> Fighting with each other as ideas take flight
Yet, gone in a second.
> Thoughts rolling around
Fighting with yourself
> It is always difficult to write.
Covered with a thin thick layer
of silken
> Delicate
>> Love and stress.
> Breaking chains
> Breaking walls
Who are you?
>> *Battered*
>>> *Beaten*
>>>> *Skin and Bones*
>>> *Insomniac*
>>>> *That maniac*
> Falling in new places
>>>> *All Highs*
>>>>> *and Lows.*
Themes of that of themes are not
> Conjunctions function but, who are you?
>>>> *The Mad Scientist Type?*
> After all, it is always difficult to write.

Stars and moonlight

Suns and clouds alike

Trees and leaves fight

But isn't the universe inside of you,

The Mad Mad Scientist Type?

Beautiful and Pointless

They keep saying you're dead
They keep saying you're alive
They keep saying
They keep saying.
        Oh, but they don't understand you the way I do.
No one knows all of your beautiful parts
And they ignore your broken ones.
So, they stare with confusion, read you once
Put you down and walk away.
        But it is me,
                Me who loves you.
                I love all of you because
                        You are beautiful and pointless
And confusing
        And empty
                Yet fulfilling and easy.
                So when I fall
        And when my soul is weeping,
Poetry, you pick me up and dust me off and say
        "You are Beautiful and Pointless but I love you just as much."

Silk Stress

When did writing become so difficult for me?

      When did it become a chore rather than an act of passion?

When did writing become something that must be done rather than

            Something that I want to be doing?

    When?

When did writing become so difficult for me?

Am I not inspired by the events occurring?

      Not inspired by the sounds of lilac colors laying upon my ears?

        Not inspired by the lips that kiss my every fault?

Not inspired by the longing for her touch?

      When did writing become so difficult for me?

As I sit staring at my blank page, Am I lost?

Too tired?

Too drained?

      Is it something in the air?

        something in my veins?

Is it this depression that hovers over me

Or just the anxiety?

Some days, writing comes to me in my sleep.

      Most days she just lays silently

In the back of my mind

      On her pillow of adjectives

With her blanket of stress thrown over her like silk.

      On days like today

      when I ask of her not to be so difficult

She leaves me in the purgatory of white space and black ink.

A Small but, Intimate Conversation

"Tell me how you feel."
"I feel like the grass is green but not for me.
I feel like the leaves

   Falling unintentionally.
I feel like the waves in the sea
I feel like the ground that was once beneath your feet.
I feel like the sky

   When it's gray

     When it's black

   When it's blue.
I feel like the clothes you never wore and like the rain
That used to hit your 16th floor window in the middle of May.
I feel like the river, the one with all the rocks
Where We used to picnic.
I feel like the job you never got
and like your favorite shoes that have holes.
I feel like the cigarette
that used to hang from your mouth

   When you were probably 18.
I feel the way you felt when you enlisted

   And the way you felt when you came back home.
I feel like the moon when it's waxing, not waning,

   but sometimes yes, waning.

     I feel like the stars but not really stars,

      just the reflection of city lights.

I feel like your favorite shirt
The one you laughed in
The one you cried in
The one you kissed in
The one you slept in.
I feel like your smile
The one that brought light into any room.
I feel like you, even though you're not here.
I feel like me, I feel like them.
I feel like everything, how can that be?

Between Two Lungs

Most times I think of you.

For an odd reason

I write so much about you.

A being with a heart and two lungs.

Lungs that shared breaths between each other

Then released.

Released

Into the trees

the clouds

the air

the stars

the moon

And galaxies beyond.

Here I am.

As the year approaches

It feels that this wound has been reopened.

And sometimes

Just sometimes

I think it never healed.

But most times, I think of you

And I wonder how many worlds

you have seen without a body holding you back.

And I wonder, I wonder

If you're still searching

For the words that were never said

For the love that never left

For the world that I am still in
For the breath between your lungs.

I write so much about you.

Letters to My Father

Dear Dad,
I thought I would know exactly what to write
the minute I opened this book.
I wanted to be direct with you, get straight to it
to all the things I never said.
People keep telling me I have to *let you go*
but I don't know anything anymore.

       Dear Dad,

              I wanted today to be different.

              I wanted to get out of the house.

              I wanted to call you.

              I wanted to let go of you but today is hard.

Dear Dad,
It is 12:18
Midnight.
I'm looking at your pictures
It hurts to write about you sometimes.

       Dear Dad,

     Day 16 of letting you go is a little easier than

             Day 15

             Day 14

             Day 10

             Day 3

            I started a new Antidepressant
They say I have "Severe Depression"

             My girlfriend says they have made me worse.

But I want to be better.

Why can't I be better, Dad?

She said to me

"You are not yourself.

I don't want to lose you

I can see it and I don't want to lose you."

Heart breaking

Heart aching

Teary eyed and the train stops.

I don't want to lose me either.

Until Next Time, I love you

Dear Dad,

It was grandma's birthday today.

February 26th.

I did not know so many people would care about her.

They didn't care for you

Why is that?

They walked past me

They talked at me.

They kept calling my girlfriend, my friend.

I know Grandma doesn't understand it either.

No one understands it.

 I pictured you everywhere

on the couch

at the table

in the mirror

in the kitchen

in front of the window.

It has been difficult.

Dear Dad,

My therapist said to me

"Grief is the price we pay for loving someone"

And I loved you.

        Dear Dad,

Were you ever in love?

Did you ever find your soulmate?

Did you love mom?

It's like she doesn't even miss you.

Everyone just keeps moving.

Do you think the woman you loved would be grieving?

        Do you feel like you lived your life?

           When you cried that night

Was it because you knew

        It would be the last time you saw me?

And when I wiped away your tears

        Did you feel how much I cared?

And when I stayed the night

        Holding your hand

           Begging you not to go

Did you already know?

        I'm writing from such a weird place, Dad.

        It has been a whirlwind since you left.

I miss you

Today

Tomorrow

Next week

Next month

Next year.

I am hesitant to state that Grandma is gone too.

How do I come back from being so fragile?

Were you fragile after the war

When you were 18 and that cigarette hung from your mouth?

Dear Dad,

Things are really weird right now.

It's been a year.

I feel like the moon

like the stars

like Jupiter

like Saturn coming out of its retrograde.

I feel like me, like you, like the universe.

I feel okay.

About the Author

Briana Roldan is a non-binary lesbian poet using gender neutral pronouns: ve, ver, vers. Ve was born and raised in New York City and resides in the Bronx with ver cat Jack as ve works towards a Bachelor's Degree in Professional and Technical Writing at the New York City College of Technology, CUNY. Briana's work takes a universal approach toward the significance of digging deeper into who we truly are as human beings through self-love and identity, sexuality, mental health, love, grief and the deeper connection we have to the universe as we accept the waves of change in all aspects of life.

A Few Thank You Notes

Firstly, thank you to my father for holding on for much longer than he could handle and for bringing me war before peace, I love you.

Thank you to my beautiful sisters and my mother for silently being there for me through writing this book.

To all my friends, you are all so much more special than I could ever express. Thank you for keeping me grounded, thank you for carrying my broken heart when it became too much. Thank you for the tearful laughs and early morning coffees and all the hugs, I love you all. I no longer want to die before you.

To my girlfriend, thank you for being one of the most supportive, most beautiful, most positive people in my life. Thank you for years of happiness and bliss, I love you.

And of course, to Carol and Jackie, I love you both so much more than I could ever write. Thank you for being my second home, thank you for all the support and understanding.

And lastly, thank you a million times over to everyone who will be reading this, everyone in the process of producing this, and to everyone who has inspired this beautiful work of art.

I truly love you all.

Headmistress Press Books

She/Her/Hers - Amy Lauren

Spoiled Meat - Nicole Santalucia

Cake - Jen Rouse

The Salt and the Song - Virginia Petrucci

mad girl's crush tweet - summer jade leavitt

Saturn coming out of its Retrograde - Briana Roldan

i am this girl - Gina Bernard

Week/End - Sarah Duncan

My Girl's Green Jacket - Mary Meriam

Nuts in Nutland - Mary Meriam, Hannah Barrett

Lovely - Lesléa Newman

Teeth & Teeth - Robin Reagler

How Distant the City - Freesia McKee

Shopgirls - Marissa Higgins

Riddle - Diane Fortney

When She Woke She Was an Open Field - Hilary Brown

God With Us - Amy Lauren

A Crown of Violets - Renée Vivien tr. Samantha Pious

Fireworks in the Graveyard - Joy Ladin

Social Dance - Carolyn Boll

The Force of Gratitude - Janice Gould

Spine - Sarah Caulfield

Diatribe from the Library - Farrell Greenwald Brenner

Blind Girl Grunt - Constance Merritt

Acid and Tender - Jen Rouse

Beautiful Machinery - Wendy DeGroat

Odd Mercy - Gail Thomas

The Great Scissor Hunt - Jessica K. Hylton